Dorothy Dase
('07)

THE DWELLING OF
THE LIGHT

Rowan Williams is the Archbishop of Canterbury
and a distinguished theologian, having been
Lady Margaret Professor of Theology at Oxford and
Dean of Clare College, Cambridge.

THE DWELLING
OF THE LIGHT

Praying with Icons
of Christ

ROWAN WILLIAMS

William B. Eerdmans Publishing Company
Grand Rapids, Michigan / Cambridge, U.K.

Text © Rowan Williams 2003

First published 2003 in the U.K. by
The Canterbury Press, Norwich

This edition published 2004 in the U.S.A. by
Wm. B. Eerdmans Publishing Company
255 Jefferson Ave. S.E., Grand Rapids, Michigan 49503
www.eerdmans.com

Printed in Denmark

08 07 06 05 04   5 4 3 2 1

ISBN 0-8028-2778-0

Designed and typeset by Vera Brice
Cover design by Leigh Hurlock

A list of illustration credits appears on page 87

Contents

THE DWELLING
OF THE LIGHT

Preface

Like an earlier small volume of reflections on icons of Mary, this book began as meditations given to various audiences during retreats and quiet days. I should specially like to thank those who invited me to lead days of prayer at the Abbey House in Glastonbury and at St Stephen's, Westbourne Park in London during 2002, as the following pages took their first shape in preparation for these events. My thanks also to Christine Smith of Canterbury Press, who encouraged me to write them out more fully; and to all those who have helped me over the years to understand the process by which an icon comes to be, particularly Mariamna Fortounatto, whose icon of the Pantocrator in the chapel of Westcott House, Cambridge, was and is for me and many others a profoundly significant image.

Canterbury
Pentecost 2003

Introduction

The Bible is very sceptical – to put it mildly – about visual images of God: the Ten Commandments forbid God's people to create carved models of the God of Israel like the images of neighbouring cultures, and the prophetic words of the Second Isaiah contain some savage satire against those who imagine that things they have themselves made can save or help them. In the days of the early Church, one of the things that most surprised non-Christians about Christian worship and places of worship was the lack of images of divine beings; for most people in that age and area, a place of worship was *essentially* a house for images of the gods. Christians must be atheists, they thought, since they had no gods around.

Yet, slowly and steadily, Christian art developed. By the sixth century, places of worship were heavily decorated with painting and mosaic (and embroidered curtains), and pictures on wooden panels were beginning to appear, showing Jesus or his mother or one or more of the saints. These images were increasingly treated with veneration and regarded as instruments for God's work.

Then, in the eighth century, there was a violent reaction in the Eastern Christian world – perhaps prompted by the claim of Islam to represent a purer and higher form of religious faith. Successive emperors in Constantinople tried to stamp out the veneration of holy images; many were destroyed, and those people who refused to co-operate were punished with great cruelty. But the crisis passed; new rulers changed the policy, and the Eastern Church defined what it believed about holy images and the veneration due to them with great care and precision.

This was not just a case of the government or the hierarchy giving in to popular superstition and accepting idolatry. The defenders of images (and 'icon' is simply the Greek word for 'image') had to produce a careful argument to show not only that these images were not the sort of thing condemned in the Bible, but that they were actually a natural consequence of the way the God of the Bible worked. It was a bold strategy, but it worked; and it worked because it was so closely connected with the most essential beliefs of Christians about Jesus Christ himself.

So when we look at icons of Christ, we are seeing what people in the eighth century saw as the test case for the rightness of having any images at all.

If anything else can be represented on the walls of a church or on a wooden panel in a house or wherever, it's because of what is believed about Jesus.

Those who attacked the use of images argued like this: Jesus is God made human; but God, as the Bible says, can't be seen and can't be painted. God, the maker of everything, is not an object like other objects in the world, but is infinite, and so impossible to show or point to in any ordinary way. If you claim you have produced a picture of God, you are in fact denying that God is really God, you're making God *less* than he truly is.

But, said the defenders of images, God became truly human in Jesus: he may have been beyond all limit in his eternal being, but he limited (or 'circumscribed') himself in Jesus. And if Jesus was indeed truly human, we can represent his human nature as with any other member of the human race.

Ah yes, said the opponents – but how can you represent his human nature alone without somehow suggesting that you can separate off his humanity from the divine life that lived in it? The Church had decided (in 451, at a council in Chalcedon) that we had to treat the divine life and the human life in Jesus as utterly inseparable. If you made an image of Jesus, you were either trying to show what God looks like, which is impossible, or you're showing what the man Jesus looked like without showing the divine life in him, and that would be to show something quite false.

The point is, though, said the defenders, that while the divine life in Jesus is indeed inseparable from the human, it acts on the human nature, shows itself through it, transfigures it. If we paint a picture of Jesus, we're not trying to show a humanity apart from divine life, but a humanity soaked through with divine life. The workings of God, the 'energy' of God, to use a favourite word of Eastern theologians, are all the time acting on and in the human nature of Jesus. We don't depict just a slice of history when we depict Jesus; we show a life radiating the light and force of God. And this means also that if we know what we're doing when we represent Jesus, if we approach the whole matter in prayer and adoration, the image that is made becomes in turn something that in its own way radiates this light and force.

And this was the argument that won the day, and that has ever since been the foundation for the way Eastern Christians understand icons. Icons are never portraits, attempts to give you an accurate representa-

tion of some human situation or some human face as
you normally see it. They are – like all our efforts in
Christian living – human actions that seek to be open
to God's action. It sounds a bit strange to call a picture an 'action' in this way; but creating an icon is
after all something 'performed' in a fixed way, with
the proper preparation of fasting and prayers, in the
hope not that you will produce a striking visual image
but that your work will open a gateway for God. Just
as God works through the human person or event
you are painting, you, responding prayerfully to that
earlier working by God, seek to allow it to continue in
and through your response.

It helps to explain why Eastern Christians are so
unhappy about statues in church – which they
do indeed think of as incompatible with the
Commandments. A statue is very clearly an object
that takes up a three-dimensional space; you can walk

round it. An icon is a surface: you can't walk round it but only look at it, and, hopefully, through it. It insists that you don't treat it as an object with which you share a bit of space. In the icon, what you see is human beings and situations as they are in the light of God's action. When you draw a diagram or even a map, you have to pick out the elements of the view that you need in order to convey what this drawing is for; it is a bit like that with an icon. It doesn't seek for photographic realism; like the lines of a diagram, the lines of an icon tell you what it is in the subject matter that is significant, that conveys God's working. And you need to look and pray with that in mind, to look patiently and not analytically, and allow yourself to be 'worked on' – perhaps we should say, allow yourself to be looked at by God, rather than just looking at something yourself.

That's why the use of icons is not some kind of image worship. Certainly icons are treated with reverence – people bow to them, kiss them, light candles in front of them and so on. Some people may approach this in a superstitious spirit, as with any practice performed in church. But the reverence – as any Eastern Christian will tell you – is not because the icons are seen as magical objects but because in their presence you become aware that you are present to God and that God is working on you by his grace, as he does in the lives and words of holy people, supremely in the words of Scripture and the person of Jesus.

And because the whole rationale is so much bound up with what Christians believe about the person of Jesus, icons depicting the Saviour are of special interest. In these short meditations, we shall be looking at icons of some of the events in the life of Jesus, but also at how he is depicted as judge of the world and ruler of all, and as one of the eternal Trinity. What we are looking at and thinking about here is simply what Christians would see as the basis for a transformed vision of the world in the transfigured and transfiguring reality of Jesus; so it makes sense to begin by looking at the icon of Jesus' transfiguration on the mountain in the presence of his disciples.

The
Transfiguration

The Eastern Christian representation of this event has been much the same for nearly a thousand years; it is one of the most dramatic and distinctive images in the tradition. Christ, his robes pure white, stands on a rocky outcrop – often his feet do not actually touch the ground. He is placed against a background of darker colour, red or deep blue or both, in concentric circles or oval 'mandorla' shapes or, especially in later versions, stars or similar geometrical patterns. Moses and Elijah stand on peaks of rock one on each side, and further down the very steep and craggy mountain are the disciples, sprawled in disorder. In late medieval examples, they often look as if they have been physically thrown down from the higher slopes.

Peter, on the left, raises one hand to cover his face,
John, in the middle, crouches on his knees, with a
hand to his face, James is often pictured flat on his
back or slipping down on his face. The sheer energy
of the portrayal is extraordinary, even in the more
monumental versions of the earlier Middle Ages.

The dark background against which Jesus is shown is
something you will see in other icons as a way of rep-
resenting the depths of heavenly reality. In the transfiguration, what the disciples see is, as you might say,
Jesus' humanity 'opening up' to its inner dimensions.
It is rather like the Hindu story of the infant Krishna,
told by his mother to open his mouth to see if he has
been eating mud; she looks in, and sees the whole
universe in the dark interior of his throat. So the
disciples look at Jesus, and see him as *coming out*
from an immeasurable depth; behind or within him,

infinity opens up, 'the dwelling of the light', to borrow the haunting phrase from Job 38.19. Mark 1.38 reports Jesus as saying that he has 'come out' so that he can proclaim the good news; and John's Gospel too uses the language of coming out from the depths of the Father (John 16.27–30). Belief in Jesus is seeing him as the gateway to an endless journey into God's love. The often-noted fact that icons show the lines of perspective reversed, so that they converge on your eye, not on a vanishing point in the distance within the picture, is a way of telling us that, once again, what is true of Jesus lies at the heart of all this style of painting: we are being taught to look through into the deep wells of life and truth.

Here, then, in Jesus is neither a human life that simply points to the divine (many lives do that), nor a supernatural visitation that is not grounded in the life we share on earth. And that's precisely the theological point. When we listen to a great instrumental performer or singer, we can sometimes sense that all their energy and life at the moment of performance is held and sustained by the great current of music that is becoming present and immediate in their actions; you can't separate them from the movement of the music, their present reality, muscles and nerves and breath and mind, is shot through with the music's 'life'. They are carried on its tide. That's a small and inadequate analogy for what this image is saying: Jesus' human life is shot through with God's, he is carried on the tide of God's eternal life, and borne towards us on that tide, bringing with him all the fullness of the creator. No wonder the disciples are sprawling helplessly; they face a tidal wave.

The whole history of God's dealings with his people is involved in this: Moses and Elijah are also driven towards us by the same energy. But Jesus alone stands in the very heart of it, it flows through him and from him. It is the light that comes from him that is reflected on the robes of his companions. They lived hundreds of years before him, yet what makes them radiant, what makes them agents of God, is the light

coming from Jesus, so that this icon – like the story it illustrates – confuses our ordinary sense of time. In the Gospels, the transfiguration story is introduced with the apparently innocent words, 'after six days' (in Matthew and Mark), or 'after about eight days' (in Luke). From early times, commentators have said that this is an allusion to the days of creation: the transfiguration is the climax of the creative work of God, either the entrance into the joy and repose of the seventh day or the beginning of the new creation, the eighth day, depending on what kind of symbolism you want to use. In Jesus, the world of ordinary prosaic time is not destroyed, but it is broken up and reconnected, it works no longer just in straight lines but in layers and spirals of meaning. We begin to understand how our lives, like those of Moses and Elijah, may have meanings we can't know of in this present moment: the real depth and significance of what we say or do now won't appear until more of the light of Christ has been seen. And so what we think is crucially important may not be so; what we think insignificant may be what really changes us for good or evil. Christ's light alone will make the final pattern coherent, for each one of us as for all human history. And that light shines on the far side of the world's limits, the dawn of the eighth day. When Jesus is transfigured, it is as if there is a brief glimpse of the end of all things – the world aflame with God's light.

In the strength of that glimpse, things become possible. We can confront today's business with new thoughts and feelings, reflect on our sufferings and our failures with some degree of hope – not with a nice and easy message of consolation but with the knowledge that there is a depth to the world's reality and out of that comes the light which will somehow connect, around and in Jesus Christ, all the complex, painful, shapeless experience of human beings. The Orthodox hymns for the feast of the Transfiguration make the point often made by Orthodox theologians: Peter, James and John are allowed to see Christ's glory so that when they witness his anguish and death they may know that these terrible moments are freely

embraced by the God-made-human who is Jesus, and held within the infinite depth of life. It is surely not an accident that it is Peter and James and John who are also with Jesus in Gethsemane: the extreme mental and spiritual agony that appears there is the test of what has been seen in the transfiguration. We are shown that God can be God even in the very heart of human terror: the life of Jesus is still carried along by the tidal wave of that which the dark background of glowing blues and reds in the icon depicts, the life of God.

This is an icon of quite violent force, explosive quality; it shows an extreme experience. We may find it difficult to relate to at first for that reason: we may be struck and impressed by it, yet feel also that nothing in our own experience corresponds to this. We weren't there; we haven't seen the skies opening, the light suffusing the lonely figure on the rock, the weight of divine presence forcing us back, bowing us down. But the point of this, as of any icon, is not either to depict or to produce some kind of special experience in that sense: it is to open our eyes to what is true about Jesus and the saints. And what is true about Jesus is – if we really encounter it in its fullness – shocking, devastating: that this human life is sustained from the depths of God without interruption and without obstacle, that it translates into human terms what and who God the Son eternally is. The shock comes from realizing this means that God's life is *compatible* with every bit of human life, including the inner terrors of Gethsemane (fear and doubt) and the outer terrors of Calvary (torment and death). We'll see later on how this theme appears also in the icons of Christ's resurrection. But the point of this image of the transfiguration is to reinforce how the truth about Christ interrupts and overthrows our assumptions about God and about humanity.

Looking at Jesus seriously changes things; if we do not want to be changed, it is better not to look too hard or too long. The apostles in the icon are shielding their eyes, because what they see is not easily manageable in their existing world. As the Eastern Christian tradition has regularly said, the light that flows from Jesus here is not a 'created' light – it isn't a phenomenon of this world, caused by factors within the universe, but a direct encounter with the action of God which alters the whole face of creation precisely because it isn't just another thing in creation. And Peter, James and John are not ready to see things with and in the light of God, any more than we are. If we ask why exactly this new perspective is so alarming, it seems to have something to do with two major insights. First: there is a solid portion of our world, the world of matter and time, which is radically open to God: the fact of Jesus' history, part of our history, is a doorway into the endlessness of God's life and resource. To recognize this is to recognize that the world of matter and time is not finally and authoritatively closed on itself; the boundaries are unsettled. In Jesus, they are, it seems, completely broken down; but this means that they are always vulnerable to God's action. The created universe may be a generally regular place; we can predict and understand how things are and will be. But this cannot be the last word. In relation to God, there is no finally closed door in creation, and the environment becomes charged with possibilities we don't know about. It is a stimulus to wonder and a warning against thinking that the world around us can be mastered once and for all and put to work for us without any problems.

But, second, there is the connection of the icon, the festival and the story with the end of Jesus' earthly life. God can live in the middle of death. That is good news on one level; on another, it means that living with God will not spare us trial, agony and death. In the Gospels, when Jesus has received Peter's admission of faith – 'You are the Anointed, the Son of the Living God' – he immediately goes on to predict his betrayal and death, and Peter protests. It is as if, there as here, he lifts his hand to his eyes because he can't manage what he sees. If only the vision of glory spared us suffering! But on the contrary, glory can only be seen for what it really is when we see it containing and surviving disaster. It has been said that St John's Gospel has no transfiguration story because the whole gospel is a transfiguration story, with its repeated emphasis that glory culminates in the cross. A huge hope, but also a huge dose of unwelcome reality: to be brought into such relation with Jesus that we live in his glory (John 17.22ff.) ought surely to mean that we are kept safe, taken out of the world. But faith in Jesus appears to mean that we have to live in the world with all its risks, our lives open to the depths from which Jesus lives.

That's what will sink in if and as we look at Jesus transfigured. We must be prepared to be mentally and spiritually flung backwards, baffled in finding adequate words for this, even fearful at the prospect of discipleship it puts before us. But it is the one vision that allows us to see everything in our experience as open to God – so that we need not fear that God is bound to disappear if we encounter this or that situation, that it is impossible to stay with God in times of failure, pain or self-doubt. That is not a glib reassurance but a sober statement of what's implied in recognizing the glory of God in Jesus.

So as we look at this icon and let it shape our prayers and reflections, we can think first of that infinite 'hinterland' that is the background, the inner dimension, of Jesus' human life. It doesn't stop being human in any sense; but it is a humanity which in every moment 'performs' God's own life. When we see that, we see that every act and suffering of Jesus is part of the act of God, embraced freely in God's journey towards us out of his depths. We can also think of how the shape of our own lives is finally going to be in God's hands, not ours: like Moses and Elijah, we don't know yet (in St John's words) what we shall be. Our time, our stories about ourselves, our histories are the best we can do from where we stand and look; but God's perspective can do strange things with history, and we are not the best judges of the meanings of our lives, what really matters to God, what shows

God to the world. But we are given a glimpse of what God can do in this rare moment of direct vision, when the 'door of perception' is opened by and in Jesus, and the end of the world is fleetingly there before us. And finally, we can let ourselves contemplate the fact that the divine freedom shown us in this vision tells us both that there is no escape from the world in which we have been put as creatures *and* that there is nowhere from which God can be finally exiled. This is the great challenge to faith: knowing that Christ is in the heart of darkness, we are called to go there with him. In John 11, Thomas says to the other disciples, 'Let us go and die with him'; and ahead indeed lies death – the dead Lazarus decaying in the tomb, the death of Jesus in abandonment, your death and mine and the deaths of countless human beings in varying kinds of dark night. But if we have seen his glory on the mountain, we know at least, whatever our terrors, that death cannot decide the boundaries of *God's* life. With him the door is always open, and no one can shut it.

The
Resurrection

The open door is at the heart of the most familiar Eastern icon of the resurrection: it shows not the moment when Jesus actually rose from the tomb, but his descent among the dead, breaking down the doors of the underworld. Orthodox theologians have said – surely rightly – that the *moment* of resurrection could not be depicted, any more than you could depict the moment of creation or the moment of incarnation. You cannot paint a picture of the simple act of God (the critics of icon worship were right about that). You can only show the effect of God's action: the creation itself carrying the mystery of God in its very being, the human situation transformed by God. So you can depict the risen Christ – there are icons of the scene in Matthew 28 where the risen Jesus meets the women who have come to anoint him – but not the event of resurrection. There are a few late examples of something like this, but these are Western-influenced works with no distinctive Eastern features.

So the classical Easter icon (the first examples of which come from the sixth century) shows something more than an historical event: it shows, you might say, the effect of God's action on human history up to that point, and, implicitly, the effect of God's action on all history. Just as the transfiguration icon shows the light of Jesus' presence illuminating Moses and Elijah, this icon shows Jesus bringing Adam and Eve out of the realm of death into that same light-filled presence. He stands in the centre of the composition, usually, once again, framed by a darker mandorla or

concentric circles of deep colour. Beneath his feet are
the shattered gates of hell (sometimes broken chains
and padlocks are scattered around as well); but most
commonly Christ is shown standing on a narrow
bridge of rock spanning a dark pit (in which you can
sometimes see the figure of the defeated Satan). In
the earlier versions, he carries a cross, and extends a
hand to lift the aged Adam from his tomb; sometimes
he holds a scroll (containing the good news to be
proclaimed to the spirits in prison, as in 1 Peter
3.19). But in the later style, especially after the

fourteenth century, he is usually grasping Adam with one hand and Eve with the other. On either side, behind Adam and Eve, stand characters from the history of Jewish Scripture, usually David and Solomon and the prophets (including, in some versions, John the Baptist).

So this is a picture of liberation. As in the transfiguration icon, Jesus comes out of the depths of divine life, out of the glowing darkness behind his white-clad figure, bringing the immediate presence of divine activity into the furthest depths of human experience. We talk in the Church's tradition about the 'Descent into Hell'; but this is not quite what the theology behind this icon means. Adam and Eve and David and Solomon and Isaiah and the Baptist are not in 'hell' in the sense that they are for ever cut off from God; but those who have lived before Christ, even those who have led saintly lives, are imprisoned, unfulfilled. The grip of death holds them; their growth towards God has been halted. The heritage of sin in the world has left them unable to encounter God with the fullness that God wants for them, and so they are left finally under the dominion of the enemy of the human race, the 'Prosecutor' (which is what 'Satan' originally meant, as Revelation 12.10 reminds us). This is not a story about Christ coming to deliver those who have deliberately said no to God, those in 'hell' in the strict sense, which raises some different questions. It is about Christ coming to those who, after all their struggle and even their attainment, after all their partial encounters with God, are stuck in the agony of knowing God a little but having been 'frozen' by death in this tantalizing half-knowledge; seeing something of God yet not being free to live with him.

And this is the state of human beings so long as they have not met with Christ. It is when his hand touches us that something new becomes possible, and we are able to become human and to live fully in God's company. But it is not just a gentle touch bestowed from on high; the drama of this scene depicts an action of God which moves 'through' death and its frustration into the place where human beings languish in their frozenness. By Jesus' death, death itself ceases to have the power to halt us in our growth.

Among those things that hold us back is our isolation from each other; by our obsession with our individual selves, we shut out what others may give us, even when they are offering life and newness. And one of the most dramatic ways we do this is by projecting blame on each other: it's often been said that the first visible effect of the fall of Adam in the story in Genesis is his eagerness to blame Eve. But it is wider than that. somehow we cut ourselves off from all sorts of sources of life. In relations between men and women, our greediness and impatience can ruin the gifts God wants to give through faithfulness and mutual service. In the relations between humanity and its natural environment, a similar greed and haste prevents us from responding to that environment with praise or wonder. We set up oppositions between soul and body, as if we could think about the health and goodness of the one without the other. In short, we are compulsive dividers, separators, and in these divisions we deny ourselves the life God is eager to give.

Some of the theologians of the Eastern Church, not long before the controversies over icons broke out, had begun to think what it meant to see Christ as the one who bridged all these divisions. Maximus the Confessor, probably the greatest Christian thinker of the seventh century, speaks of how every one of the great separations human beings have got used to is overcome in the person and the action and the suffering of Jesus. The divide between man and woman, between paradise before the fall and the earth as we now know it, between heaven and earth, between the mind's knowledge and the body's experience, between creature and creator – all are overcome in the renewed humanity that Christ creates.

The details of Maximus' picture are complex, and it is unlikely that any later icon painter had anything quite like this in mind; but there is something in the icon of the resurrection that fits with this vision. Christ stands on a precarious-looking bridge, as if he is the one who by the great risks and pains of his incarnation connects what we have pulled apart. And in those icons where we see him reaching out simultaneously to Adam and Eve, it is as if he is reintroducing them to each other after the ages of alienation and bitterness that began with the recriminations of Genesis. The resurrection is a moment in which human beings are reintroduced to each other across the gulf of mutual resentment and blame; a new

human community becomes possible. And similarly,
remembering the other figures from the first covenant
in the background of the picture, we realize that this
community is unaffected by any division between the
living and the dead: David and Solomon, Abraham,
Moses, Elijah and Isaiah are our contemporaries
because of Jesus' resurrection.

This suggests, incidentally, something about how we read the Bible as Christian believers. The Bible is not a human record from the distant past, full of a mixture of inspiring and not-so-inspiring stories or thoughts; nor is it a sort of magical oracle, dictated by God. It is rather the utterances and records of human beings who have been employed by God to witness to his action in the world, now given to us by God so that we may learn who he is and what he does; and the 'giving' by God is by means of the resurrection of Jesus. The risen Jesus takes hold of the history of God's people from its remotest beginnings, lifts it out of death by bringing it to completeness, and presents it to us as his word, his communication to us here and now. Because we live in the power of the risen Christ, we can hear and understand this history, since it is made contemporary with us; in the risen Christ,

David and Solomon, Abraham and Moses, stand in the middle of our assembly, our present community, speaking to us about the God who spoke with them in their lifetimes in such a way that we can see how their encounter with God leads towards and is completed in Jesus. In the Fourth Gospel, Jesus speaks of Abraham being glad to see his coming (John 8.56); this is the thought that the icon represents. Just as Jesus reintroduces Adam and Eve as he takes each of them by the hand, so he takes Abraham and ourselves by the hand and introduces us to each other. And from Abraham we learn something decisive about faith, about looking to an unseen future and about trusting that the unseen future has the face of Christ. Thus a proper Christian reading of the Bible is always a reading that looks and listens for that wholeness given by Christ's resurrection; if we try to read any passage without being aware of the light of the resurrection, we shall read inadequately.

The resurrection, then, is to do with the creation of the new humanity, where resentment and hostility are 'unfrozen'; and with the establishment of scriptural revelation as a living relationship within this new humanity. It is the foundation for understanding both Church and Bible. But if we also bear in mind the context in which Maximus the Confessor sets the work of Christ, we can see here in outline the foundation for understanding the relation of Church and creation. The resurrection in principle does away with those factors that frustrate and distort our relation as human beings with our environment – our human and historical environment, all those who have gone before us (Abraham and Moses), but also our natural environment. If the Risen Christ takes hold of and speaks through the great figures of biblical history, can we say that by the same token he speaks through the world around us? That he introduces us to that world and requires us to listen to it and receive from it what he wants to communicate?

Certainly this is to go further than the icon itself; yet it is a very obvious consequence both of the theology that shows Christ uniting what fallenness and sin have separated and of the image of a whole history being brought to fulfilment. The same insight is at work here as we found in the transfiguration icon. What Christ does and suffers affects all things, all areas of human experience and so all aspects of human relation, including relation with what is not human. Around him the whole universe reorganizes itself, just as human history reorganizes itself around this new centre which is at the same time the ancient unchangeable centre of God's glory. Once again, the Jesus who lived and died as a particular human being 'opens out' upon the glory of God. And that glory is here visually brought down into the middle of the realm of death so that death may be swallowed up.

As his hand grasps the hands of Adam and Eve, Jesus goes back to embrace the first imaginable moment of rebellion and false direction in human life – as in the icons and liturgy of the transfiguration we are reminded that he goes fully into the depths of human agony. He reaches back to and beyond where human memory begins: 'Adam and Eve' stand for wherever it is in the human story that fear and refusal of God began – not a moment we can date in ordinary history, any more than we can date in the history of each one of us where we began to forget God. But we are always dealing with the after-effects of that moment, both as a human race and as particular persons. The icon declares that wherever that lost moment is or was, Christ has been there, to implant the possibility, never destroyed, of another turning, another future; in his resurrection, he brings all those possibilities to reality.

Looking at this, then, we can first of all be sure that Christ has chosen to accompany us from the first point at which we began to lose our faithfulness to God; that he has been there at the roots of whatever sin and self-destructiveness we have been involved in;

and that he has already sown in us the seeds that will come to new life. How they do depends on whether we are willing to put our trust in him as the one in whose company we come fully to life.

We can see too how the Bible is the record of those who have come fully to life with Christ. They begin their journey towards life through the workings of God in the history of what we know as the Old Testament; but in relation with the story of Jesus we can see most fully where God was and is at work in them. We can distinguish clearly between their failures and frustrations and the moments where they are really transparent to God. The light of Jesus shows us where in their lives to see the highlights and the shadows. They can be seen as rounded persons in relation to him. And we know them now as contemporaries, speaking to us today in witness to the Christ they rejoice to see.

We are also pressed here to look at where we most deeply experience division, the different kinds of dividedness that Maximus speaks of. We must examine what there is of resentment, lack of mutual respect and anxiety in our understanding of the relation between man and woman; what there is of ignorance and contempt towards the past (ours as well as other people's); what there is of greed and violence in our use of the material world. The resurrection, remember, is an *introduction* – to our buried selves, to our alienated neighbours, to our physical world. It is because of the resurrection that we can befriend all these, as Jesus takes our hands and holds them in his.

And in this, of course, we are gradually nudged

towards the central realization of all. We are brought into this friendship with the biblical revelation, with each other and with the world because the resurrection of Jesus brings us into friendship with the divine life itself. It is because the uttermost of death and humiliation cannot break the bond between Jesus and the Father that what Jesus touches is touched by the Father too. As he grasps Adam and Eve, so does the Father; as he draws together the immeasurable past with all its failures and injuries, it is the Father to whom he draws it. Because of his relation with the Father, a new relation is made possible between ourselves and this final wellspring of divine life. The Christ of this icon, standing on the bridge over darkness and emptiness, moving into the heart of human longing and incompletion, brings into that place the mystery out of which his life streams, represented in the mandorla against which his figure is set. The locked gates of death, the frozen lives cut short, these are overcome in the act of new creation which we are witnessing.

The Hospitality
of Abraham

To most modern Western Christians, probably the best-known and best-loved of all icons is the fifteenth-century Andrei Rublev's portrayal of what is often referred to as 'The Old Testament Trinity', though it is more accurately called by its traditional Eastern name, 'The Hospitality of Abraham'. From a very early date indeed, the story in Genesis 18 of the three angels who visited Abraham by the oaks of Mamre had been taken by Christians as a foreshadowing of the revelation that God is three agents sharing one agency, three irreducible 'hypostases' or subsisting realities and one substance. The angels in the story represent, we are told, an appearance of 'the Lord'; they speak and act as one. Even in the interpretation given by the Jewish philosopher Philo in the first Christian century, the story is understood as showing the supreme God appearing with the two eternal 'powers' by which he sustains and governs the universe. Christians eagerly built upon this, identifying those powers with the personal realities of the Word and the Spirit as they are revealed in the events of Jesus' life and the calling and empowering of the Christian community.

The Genesis passage later on provided an answer to a very obvious conundrum. The whole theology of icons depended upon the incarnation; God could be depicted only because God had taken and transformed ordinary flesh and blood. But the Father and the Holy Spirit had never taken flesh, and so could not be painted. Eastern religious art avoided until a very late and rather decadent stage the curious

Western habit of showing God the Father as an old man and the Spirit as a dove. Did that mean that the Trinity itself could never be depicted? In a sense, yes, it did; there could be no way of showing the eternal life of God 'in itself'. *But* there was this narrative in which it seemed that the three divine agents appeared visibly in history; here was the vehicle for some kind of representation of the mystery.

So the icon gradually takes its classical shape through the Middle Ages. Initially, the narrative is still very much in evidence: Abraham and Sarah are clearly visible, as are the trees in the landscape and the dwelling of the patriarch. But as time goes on, the details recede and painters concentrate on the three figures. Originally set side by side, identically dressed, they are later arranged around a table, the figures carefully differentiated. Rublev's version is the most 'abstract'

in terms of the narrative setting, but it should not be thought of as independent of it, and some details remain – the single tree, the portico of a house. It was recognized rapidly as a classical model and commended as the authoritative way of executing this theme.

Now it is obviously stretching things rather to approach this as an icon of Christ. It does not show the incarnate Lord, and it is risky to assume that the painter's intention was to identify each of the three figures clearly as a particular divine person. It is true that some earlier versions show the central figure as noticeably larger than the others, which may indicate that this is meant to be God the Father as source of the others. But it is, as I have already hinted, very important in the interpretation of the story that it shows three agents acting as one – not a sort of divine drama with different characters. At a time when the theology of the Trinity sometimes sounds as though we are talking about three 'personalities' collaborating in a project, it is good to be reminded forcefully that all that God does is done by the whole Trinity equally, and that to talk of three divine persons must not mislead us into thinking of human patterns of relationship and co-operation.

Yet Rublev and others give one unmistakable signal that the arrangement of the figures is significant.

Here the central angel wears a tunic of dark red or mulberry colour and a blue mantle; over his right shoulder is what was originally one of the vertical stripes which decorated an under-tunic in Roman times, but which has something of the appearance of a deacon's stole. In short, the central angel is dressed exactly as Christ is (almost invariably) dressed throughout the centuries of Eastern Christian art. While we can accept all the proper cautions about not treating the figures as simple depictions of the trinitarian persons, there is certainly a convention which understands that the icon is to be 'read' from left to right as pointing to the Father, the Son and the Spirit; more significantly, the evocation in the central figure of the normal representation of Christ seems to be telling us that the central or pivotal thing in our understanding of the Trinity must be Jesus Christ incarnate.

This is the figure around whom the composition turns. Our eyes are drawn first to this more boldly coloured focus, the hand extended over a chalice on the table (other versions make it clear that the chalice contains a slaughtered animal, as if to make us think of the sacrificial Lamb of God). But the inclination of

the head and the direction of the eyes turns us towards the figure on the left; and the curving line of the composition leads us to the third figure whose posture echoes the central figure's inclination towards the angel on the left.

As in many icons of the Virgin and Child, we learn a great deal from following where the hands and eyes lead us. And in this image, there is, quite simply, no

place to stop; the movement circles around and around. It is impossible to stand and look any of the figures in the eye: no full-face contact is possible. And this immediately says something crucial for our understanding of both Jesus and the Holy Trinity. To look at Jesus is not to enter into a simple one-to-one relation. It is right to think of Jesus as my personal Lord and Saviour, to express that in terms of loving devotion; but we need to be careful that we do not stop there. Remembering what we were thinking about in connection with the resurrection icon, we must never lose sight of the fact that the thrust, the direction of all Jesus is and does and suffers is towards the Father from whom he comes. The Word, the Son of God is in all eternity – as St John's Prologue makes plain – an active motion towards and into the depths of the Father. Jesus as the Word made flesh makes no sense at all unless we see where he is moving – hence the powerful stress in John's Gospel on Jesus as the Way. To understand Jesus and to relate rightly to Jesus is to be with him in his move-ment towards the ultimate source of divine life, the completely self-emptying love that generates this eternal answer of total attention and devotion. Human words, not at all adequate, for the mystery, but they are all we have.

Equally, though, it is not that we are brought to a static contemplation of the Father. One early

Christian writer suggested that in Christ we came to a vantage-point from which we could look into the 'abyss' of the Father's nature; but this is not enough, and it dangerously implies that there is a sort of shapeless mysteriousness beyond what is shown in Jesus. In the icon, we are drawn 'around' to the third figure who, so to speak, presses us back towards the central one by reflecting or shadowing the central figure's position. The mystery of the Father is seen or encountered through the Son, and then seen or encountered as breathing out the Spirit; and that Spirit leads nowhere but back to the Son. To look into the mystery of the Father is to be caught up in the Father's will and desire to bring the Son to life over and over again in all the various forms in which the Son's life is capable of being shared or imitated or echoed in creation. So the life of the Father is only to be understood as wholly directed to that breathing of the Spirit which makes the Son alive and real. This is what St Paul means by saying that the Spirit teaches

us to pray 'Abba, Father', to pray in a way that echoes the Son. But if we take an even broader view, as St Paul himself does in Romans 8, all creation is brought back to harmony when the Son's prayer is prayed in our world. Because the Word is also the Wisdom in which all things come to be and all things hang together, when the Word's life is fully present in the world, all things begin to reshape themselves

around him – as we saw in thinking about the resurrection icon; and this is the Spirit's doing, as the life
of the incarnate Word is kept alive in the community
and its sacraments through the Spirit's power.

The point of all this potentially rather heady vision is,
in practical terms, to tell us that the Trinity is *never* an
object (or a trio of objects!) at a safe distance.
Knowing the Trinity is being involved in this circling
movement: drawn by the Son towards the Father,
drawn into the Father's breathing out of the Spirit so
that the Son's life may be again made real in the
world. It is where contemplation and action become
inseparable.

The doctrines of Christ and of the Trinity can seem

remarkably remote and theoretical to most people these days; what we seem to forget is that they were designed in order not only to tell us the truth about God but to make us live that truth. They are *invitations*, ways of passing on Jesus' invitation to be changed, to repent and trust him, to walk with him. This image of the Trinity more than most ought to make that clear. As has often been said, the empty place at the table is for us; there is, so to speak, a fourth seat which completes the picture, and that is where we observers are. But it is not literally a place from which we can look objectively at something called the Trinity, because our eyes (and hearts) cannot but move with the movement of the figures. St Augustine once wrote of the Kingdom of Heaven as 'not just to be looked at but to be lived in', and expounded this living in the Kingdom in terms of journeying with Christ: it is the same point here. Accepting the invitation, going through the gate into the new territory of Jesus' life (and it is worth noting how often we come back to open doors of one kind and another in thinking about icons of Christ), is the essence of orthodoxy; the teachings of classical theology are there to reinforce and expound the divine welcome.

Look too at the hand extended over the chalice. Once again, it evokes the conventional image of Christ as ruler and teacher, the two first fingers extended in the classical gesture meant to command attention. But the hand is not raised, as in the more straightforward images of the Saviour; it hovers over the dish. It is as

though the real substance of what the Word of God teaches is the chalice on the table itself. What has God to say in Christ? That the creation is invited to share the table; that this invitation is made only at the cost of sacrifice and suffering, the acceptance of a cup that will not pass from Jesus (think of the prayer in Gethsemane); that our yes to this welcome commits us to the self-giving economy of God the Trinity and so to a sharing of the cross, and that in this alone is our life.

A great deal more could be and has been said about this extraordinary icon. In its refusal to give us a static place to look, it embodies more than any words could possibly do the nature of the doctrine to which it witnesses. But there is perhaps one further point worth pondering. We have granted that this is not a 'picture' of the Trinity in any ordinary way, and that the three figures are not straightforwardly portraits of the three divine persons; rather we are looking into and following the path of the divine process of dealing with us to reveal and save. And in the centre of that is the Word. What Rublev does in so plainly clothing the ageless, sexless figure of the angel with the garments of the incarnate Christ *may* (we can't say more) suggest a particular theological point. Nothing is known of God the Trinity that does not come through the Word incarnate; this is the movement we must be drawn into so as to come fully and finally to our home in God's life. Yet here is the vesture of the historical redeemer clothing a figure more than historical; is there here a reminder of some kind that we lose a dimension of full understanding if we simply and exhaustively identify the action of the Word with what we know of the historical Jesus?

There is a range of vastly difficult questions in the background here, the most obvious of which is probably to do with whether all those who come to the Father by way of the Word, by way of Jesus Christ, will have known the *face* of Jesus – the question of God's dealing with those of other faiths or even of none. I don't for a moment believe that Rublev was thinking of this; but it is worth reflecting on the way he obliges us to look, as it were, through the incarnate Lord's features – not ignoring them, not setting them aside, but acknowledging that Jesus is what we see in history of an infinite identity and reality, God the Word, the One who is next to the Father's heart. Remember the transfiguration icon, the image of the infinite hinterland opening up behind the face of Jesus. It is appropriate that we should be left by this icon with a question about who we might encounter on the way to the Father. We can say that anyone on this road is there because of the Word, even because of what Christ historically achieves in his crucifixion and resurrection, whose effects are simply there, given, accomplished for the whole creation; but on our own unending journey into the circling motion of divine love, we may well hesitate before deciding prematurely who journeys with us. We do best to hope and trust that the point comes where every traveller is able to recognize the Saviour's face, and so to know themselves as they are known.

Pantocrator

The Saviour's face: most Christians have a sort of inherited sense of what Jesus 'looks like' – the tunic and mantle, the parted hair and forked beard, the intense gaze of the eyes; and it is the image that has been shaped by nearly fifteen hundred years of representations based on the 'Pantocrator' ('Ruler of all') icon in one form or another, or on the equally ancient convention of the *acheiropoietos* image, the likeness 'made without hands'. This latter type is associated with the legend (first attested in the fourth century) of the image miraculously imprinted by the Lord himself on a napkin to be sent to the King of Edessa. Its features are much the same as the Pantocrator, but it shows only the face itself. The earliest surviving examples of panel paintings of the Pantocrator come from the sixth century (there is a superb instance from Mount Sinai executed in encaustic wax). There has been quite a bit of speculation about origins and influences – classical depictions of Zeus, the father of the gods, played some part, as did, more surprisingly, pictures of the poet Homer; but it is absolutely clear that, by the early sixth century, everyone in the Christian East, and plenty of others too, knew how to recognize Christ in images such as these.

Sometimes they are full-length representations of Christ with the apostles or martyrs; with a bishop or emperor bowing or prostrating before him; with the Mother of God and the Baptist flanking him. He is seated on an imperial throne, often with a mandorla around him, his right hand slightly raised, with the two first fingers extended, and he holds a book in his left hand. But the commonest form, in medieval frescoes and panel paintings, is probably that in which we see only the upper part of the body. By the early Middle Ages, there is a clearly settled pattern for this half-length figure – the blue overmantle and ochre tunic, the raised hand, the book normally open, and increasingly often displaying a gospel text; and by the end of the Middle Ages, almost invariably, a halo enclosing a cross, and the Greek words, *ho ōn* 'the existing one', 'he who is'. Usually the Greek abbreviation IC XC also appears (for *Iēsous Christos*).

'The existing one' is the translation in the Greek Old Testament of the Hebrew phrase in Exodus 3.13, where God names himself to Moses as 'I am who I am' or 'I am whatever I will be'. And here is the first thing to reflect on in this icon. What we see is Jesus

of Nazareth, a human figure in modest, not royal or priestly, clothing; a recognizably human face and figure. Yet of this face and figure we say, 'This is truth, this is reality'; what is alive in Jesus is life itself, the very act of being which is God. Although this human being, like any human being, is vulnerable to what happens in history (and the cross in the halo reminds us of just what that means), this human being is in every moment, even in the deepest vulnerability, *acting out the act of God*. Divine action appears to us in all the human detail of this life, not as an extra to it, not as a mysterious something or other floating above the surface of history, but embodied in it. To confront Jesus is to confront eternal truth. If, like Pontius Pilate, we ask, 'What is truth?', the answer is before us: *'He is'*. This icon is a kind of visual translation of the Gospel of John, where Jesus again and again says of himself the divine words, 'I am'.

So, quite simply, this is reality that we face; nothing is more fundamental than Jesus, nothing will bring us closer to the heart of being itself than Jesus. Whether we are looking at God, at the universe or at our own lives, the deepest level we can attain is to be found here, in confronting Jesus. The being of God, about which we can say nothing adequate at the level of theory and abstraction except the most tantalizing generalities and negations ('all-powerful', 'beyond

time and change', and so on), is, as far as we are con-
cerned, fully laid open to us in Jesus. To be in relation
with Jesus is to be 'in the truth', even when we cannot
formulate this in tidy philosophical language. And
this also tells us that there is something in the being
of God that is *appropriately* expressed in a vulnerable
life, in the self-forgetfulness that brings ultimate truth
to us in the limits of suffering and mortality. The
nature of God is both irreducibly mysterious and
completely expressed in God's putting himself
unreservedly at our disposal and our mercy in
becoming embodied in a human life.

Ho ōn, 'the existing one': existence itself is rooted in
the divine 'humility', the divine self-forgetting. So for
us to be true and real is for us to enter into that kind
of reality – not to seek for a divine dignity and knowledge that lifts us out of this messy world, but to seek

to be aligned with God's sacrificial love as we live our lives, with all the risk that involves. There is no static and detached 'divine nature' somewhere beyond the active love that is God. God is threefold relationship, God is the love that welcomes us, and there is, in one all-important sense, nothing more we need to know of God – as our reflections on Rublev's Trinity icon have already indicated.

But two other features of this icon reinforce the same point in distinct ways. The fingers of the right hand look to the modern eye as if they are blessing – and this is not wholly wrong. But originally, in classical art, such gestures were meant to identify someone engaged in *teaching*. As we noted in looking at the Trinity icon, the position of the hands is meant to signify a claim to attention. So what is also encoded in this image is the insight that truth, reality itself, is *self-*

communicating: reality 'longs' to be known, to share and instruct, to reach out and make a claim on our gaze. As some modern theologians have said, especially the great Catholic thinker, Hans Urs von Balthasar, in order for us to believe that our knowledge of anything is in some degree true, a sharing in what's there, we need to see existence itself as caught up in God's own will, God's own 'longing', to share divine truth; everything in creation is a divine outreaching to us. To know something is to become alert to God's outreach within it. In the face of Christ, we begin to learn how to look and listen for that outreach in the whole world; and we are reminded again of how all these icons of Christ are designed to make us see *everything* freshly.

And then the text in the open book: sometimes Christ is gesturing towards the book, as though to connect this particular text with his reaching out to us or to identify this as the truth which at this particular moment we need to learn about God and ourselves; in one very famous example, the terrifying mosaic in the dome at Daphni, the book is closed. The texts are often from St John's Gospel – 'I am the light of the world', 'I am the Way, the Truth and the Life', 'Do not judge according to appearances, but be just in your judgement'; though Matthew 11.28, 'Come to me all who are weary and heavy-laden', is also common. Sometimes the pages of the book simply display an alpha and omega, echoing the significance of *ho ōn*.

The iconographer will normally choose the text according to the need and circumstance of those who will regularly contemplate it, and this can be a serious challenge to prayerful discernment for the painter.

But whatever the text, the meaning is clear enough: the living Christ points to the written word of the Bible for his truth to come home to us in this or that specific moment. And the words may be inviting or challenging or reassuring, but their point is always to establish for us the relation in which we stand to

Christ: facing him and learning what is true of us and of God. When, as at Daphni, the book is closed, it is as though we are told that only Christ himself can know the real nature of this relation; we cannot 'read' the truth by our own resources, and must simply wait in his presence. But generally this image is one in which we are directed towards Scripture to reinforce the underlying statement made by the icon as a whole: reality is, finally, the love of a personal God, and the Bible is there to recall us to that revelation of the very character of the divine life, centred on Jesus, as we saw in looking at the transfiguration and resurrection icons. We meet God as 'word', as communication, in the world, in Jesus, and in the biblical record, because the action of God is always communicative, designed to transform our knowing and feeling selves. And when we approach the Bible, we must approach it as if it were, as in this icon, held open before us by the living Christ. Christians, especially in the West, are prone to two kinds of misunderstanding here – either reading the Bible as a mere record of what some human beings thought in the past, or reading it as an oracle divorced from the living personal presence of Christ, so that we don't read it in the light of Christ. Reflecting on this icon can help put our reading of the Bible into the perspective of relation with Christ, so that we read asking him to show us in our reading the truth of ourselves and God, once again.

The point is simple: face to face with Jesus, there and only there, do we find who we are. We have been created to mirror his life, the eternal life of the one turned always towards the overflowing love of the Father; but our human existence constantly turns away. When we look at Jesus, we see in some measure what he sees, and are drawn to where his eyes lead us. In the Trinity icon, we grasp how he leads us to the

mystery from which his own life eternally flows; in this icon, we look at him looking at us, and try to understand that as he looks at us he looks at the Father. In other words, when he sees us, he sees the love that is his own source and life, despite all we have done to obscure it in ourselves. When we look at him looking at us, we see both what we were made to be, bearers of the divine image and likeness, and what we have made of ourselves.

Where do his eyes lead us, then? To our own deepest reality, to the loving self-communication of God which is at the heart of our existence and which by sin and laziness and forgetfulness we deny; to the wellspring of divine life in the centre of what we are, the Word that calls us into being. Remember the wonderful ending of Charles Wesley's hymn, 'Jesu, lover of my soul': 'Spring thou up within my heart, Rise to all eternity'. That is what the eyes of Christ the Panto-crator direct us to. His gaze upon us takes us to the abiding love of the creator that is expressed in the sheer fact of our being here at all; as we look at that unchanging self-gift, we see what Jesus sees, what the Son of God sees in looking at the Father. And we begin with him to see the Father as we look at all things and persons. We see the distortions, the refusals and the tragedies, and see them all the more

80

horribly and painfully in the light; but we don't stop being able to see the gift of the maker who still loves in and through it all. The dwelling of the light is in us as well – not simply in the sense in which some speak of the 'Inner Light' which guides us, but in the radiance that all creatures contain. Jewish mysticism speaks of the Shekinah, the glorious presence of God, hidden in the world, waiting for holy people to come and set it free; some Russian writers have used the Old Testament language of 'Sophia', holy Wisdom, to name this hidden glory. But if Christ always looks at the Father, and if here in this icon he looks at us steadily and faithfully, then whatever name we use we are being drawn towards this secret fire in the heart of earthly reality.

Epilogue

In all these meditations on icons of Christ, we find ourselves looking at far more than just the representation of a human being of long ago. We are brought into the presence of one who contains everything, who makes everything hang together, who gives us the power to see all things freshly. We began by recalling the worries of those who couldn't see how you could possibly *depict* God, especially not in the depiction of a human face. But the Church concluded that this human face, showing a life that was completely the gift of God to us for our healing and forgiveness, would show us God (as St Paul says in 2 Corinthians 4.6, 'the light of the knowledge of the glory of God in the face of Jesus Christ'). It does not show us God as if he were laid out as an object for inspection; it shows God by taking us on a journey in which we discover what the relations are that have been created between us and Jesus; and as we begin to grasp what these are and what they imply, what they require of us and what they make possible for us, it is God that 'appears' as the context and the boundary of all we are thinking and saying and experiencing. As we encounter these images in thought and prayer, we are shown the way to the dwelling of the light, deeper in everything than we can ever go, further beyond everything than we can ever go – yet here, directly and simply, in the face of Jesus.